The APOLLO 11 MOON LANDING

A DAY THAT CHANGED AMERICA

by Amy Maranville

CAPSTONE PRESS
a capstone imprint

Capstone Captivate is published by Capstone Press, an imprint of Capstone.
1710 Roe Crest Drive, North Mankato, Minnesota 56003
www.capstonepub.com

Library of Congress Cataloging-in-Publication Data
Names: Maranville, Amy, author.
Title: The Apollo 11 moon landing : a day that changed America / by Amy Maranville.
Other titles: The Apollo eleven moon landing
Description: North Mankato, Minnesota : Capstone Press, [2022] | Series: Days that changed America | Includes bibliographical references and index. | Audience: Ages 8-11 | Audience: Grades 4-6 | Summary: "On July 20, 1969, Neil Armstrong took one giant leap for mankind when he became the first person to set foot on the moon. Now readers can step back in time to learn about what led up to the Apollo 11 moon landing, how the historic event unfolded, and the ways in which one remarkable day changed America forever"-- Provided by publisher.
Identifiers: LCCN 2021012646 (print) | LCCN 2021012647 (ebook) | ISBN 9781663920751 (paperback) | ISBN 9781663905758 (hardcover) | ISBN 9781663905727 (pdf) | ISBN 9781663905741 (kindle edition)
Subjects: LCSH: Project Apollo (U.S.)--Juvenile literature. | Apollo 11 (Spacecraft)--Juvenile literature. | Space flight to the moon--Juvenile literature. | Moon--Exploration--Juvenile literature. Classification: LCC TL789.8.U6 M3495 2022 (print) | LCC TL789.8.U6 (ebook) | DDC 629.45/4--dc23
LC record available at https://lccn.loc.gov/2021012646
LC ebook record available at https://lccn.loc.gov/2021012647

Image Credits
Associated Press: 19, Marty Lederhandler, 4; NASA: cover, 5, 9, 10, 11, 12, 13, 14, 15, 16, 17, 18, 20, 21, 22, 23, 24, 27, JPL-Caltech, 25; Newscom: Everett Collection, 6; Shutterstock: Atoly (design element), cover and throughout, Everett Collection, 26, Oleg Golovnev, 8, pablofdezr, 7

Editorial Credits
Editor: Eric Braun; Designer: Heidi Thompson; Media Researcher: Svetlana Zhurkin; Production Specialist: Kathy McColley

Consultant Credits
Sarah Ruiz, Aerospace Engineer

All internet sites appearing in back matter were available and accurate when this book was sent to press.

TABLE OF CONTENTS

Words in **bold** are in the glossary.

On July 20, 1969, people all over Earth were glued to their television sets. They watched in wonder as human beings landed on the moon for the first time. Then the first **astronaut** stepped out onto its surface. That footstep changed history.

While some people watched the historic Apollo 11 moon landing at home, huge crowds also gathered to view it on large outdoor TV screens.

One of the first steps taken by the American astronauts on the moon

Humans had never traveled so far from Earth. Now that we had done it, people began to dream of exploring even farther. They asked, "What else can we do?" Science began to seem fun and exciting. The moon landing inspired hope. Great things seemed possible.

CHAPTER 1

THE SPACE RACE

Starting in the late 1940s, the United States had been in a cold war against the Soviet Union. In a "cold war," armies do not fire weapons. Instead, the countries build bigger and bigger weapons. They spy on each other. They try to create better technology.

The Soviet Union successfully sent a rocket to the moon in 1959. To mark this victory, Soviet leader Nikita Khrushchev (right) presented President Eisenhower (second from right) with a gift.

The United States and the Soviet Union did all these things. They also tried to out do each other exploring space. This was called the "space race."

THE SOVIET UNION

The Soviet Union was the largest country in the world. It was also one of the most powerful. Its largest republic was Russia. Russia was home to its capital of Moscow. The Soviet Union fell apart in 1991 and was split into many countries.

The Soviet Union was made of 15 republics that became independent countries in 1991.

At first, the Soviet Union was winning the space race. It was the first to orbit Earth with a satellite. A Soviet **cosmonaut**, Yuri Gagarin, became the first human to orbit Earth in 1961. The United States space program had many failures. The United States was worried.

FACT

Cosmonaut is the Russian word for "astronaut."

A Soviet newspaper praised Yuri Gagarin's space flight as a great achievement for all people.

In 1962, President Kennedy inspired Americans to support the Apollo space program.

Then U.S. President John F. Kennedy made an announcement. He said that America would reach the moon before the end of the 1960s. He repeated this promise in September 1962. He said, "We choose to go to the moon in this decade."

The United States worked even harder on the space race. The National Aeronautics and Space Administration (NASA) put its finest minds on the project. Scientific discovery became a national focus.

CHAPTER 2

LIFTOFF!

NASA brought in new teams of astronauts. A group that started in 1962 was nicknamed the New Nine. Among them was Neil Armstrong. He was a former navy pilot and civilian test pilot. Fourteen more astronauts were announced in 1963. This group included Edwin "Buzz" Aldrin. He was an air force pilot who had studied rockets and spacecraft. It also included air force pilot Michael Collins. These three became the crew of the Apollo 11.

Neil Armstrong (left), Michael Collins (center), and Buzz Aldrin (right) worked together to prepare for the first manned lunar landing mission.

NASA AND DIVERSITY

The most visible NASA workers were white and male. But women and people of color worked behind the scenes. They were a big part of Apollo's success. They did calculations and managed communications. They even sewed space suits. NASA needed all the best minds. That meant hiring people who were often held back by their gender or race.

NASA research mathematician Katherine Johnson was one of many people who contributed to the success of the U.S. space program out of public view.

Apollo 11 had three pieces. Columbia was the **command module**. This was the core of the ship. The inside was about as big as the inside of a car. The astronauts would work and live there.

The **service module** managed **life support** for the astronauts. It carried important things like oxygen and water. It also provided the power Columbia needed to run.

The **lunar module** (LM) was the spacecraft the astronauts would take down to the moon. It was lightweight. It held cameras and storage for moon rocks. The LM's official name was Eagle.

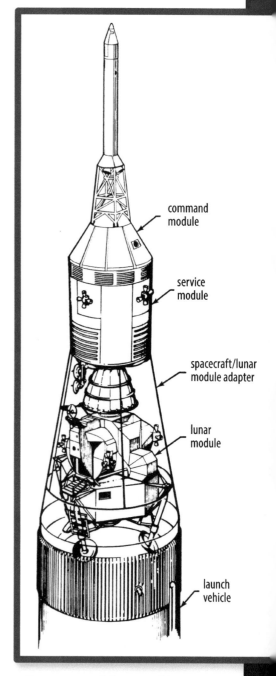

command module

service module

spacecraft/lunar module adapter

lunar module

launch vehicle

Diagram of the Apollo spacecraft set up for launch

Finally the big day arrived: July 16, 1969. A giant rocket called Saturn V was moved onto a launchpad in Cape Canaveral, Florida. The rocket was 363 feet (111 meters) tall. That's taller than the Statue of Liberty! Apollo 11 was attached to it. The crew climbed inside.

A special carrier slowly moved the Saturn V rocket to the launchpad.

About 1 million people gathered to watch the launch. They were on beaches and highways in the area. Millions more around the world followed on TV or the radio. They wanted to witness one of the most daring experiments in world history.

FACT
Technology has advanced a lot since 1969. A 2019 iPhone has about 7 million times more memory than the computer that controlled Apollo 11.

American and international reporters watched the launch from the press site.

Apollo 11 liftoff

The rocket rumbled to life. Fire and smoke blew out the bottom. Apollo 11 shook like there was an earthquake. At 9:32 a.m., Saturn V lifted off. It roared in the astronauts' ears. They were slammed back in their seats. The rocket pushed the ship up through Earth's atmosphere.

When the astronauts reached outer space, all the pressure disappeared. Their arms and legs felt light in the weightlessness of space. The Saturn V rocket broke away from Apollo 11. The mission was underway.

CHAPTER 3

THE MOON WALK

It took the astronauts four days to reach the moon. Then it was time for Armstrong and Aldrin to go down to the moon's surface. They said goodbye to Michael Collins. He would stay on Columbia.

The LM took Neil Armstrong and Buzz Aldrin to the moon's surface.

Sea of Tranquility

FACT

The Sea of Tranquility is an area of the moon that looks smooth and calm from Earth. Though it is called a sea, there is no water.

At first, things went well. The LM broke away from Columbia. The ship's computer controlled the flight. It moved them down to the moon. They were supposed to land on the moon's Sea of Tranquility. NASA thought it would be clear and smooth. But as the astronauts got closer, they saw big rocks everywhere. It wasn't safe to land there.

Charles Duke Jr. (left) closely followed communications from Apollo 11 astronauts as they lowered down to the moon's surface.

Armstrong took control of piloting from the computer. He had to find a smooth spot to land. To find one, he had to fly the LM much farther than they had planned. This left them very low on fuel. If he took too long, they would run out. Mission Control counted down the seconds before they would have to cancel the landing. Finally, Armstrong managed to land the LM on the moon's surface. Neil Armstrong announced, "The Eagle has landed."

The NASA team members on Earth had been very worried. Now they were relieved. Mission controller Charles Duke Jr. summed up their feelings. "You've got a bunch of guys about to turn blue," he told Armstrong. "We're breathing again."

About 600 million people around the world sat around black-and-white televisions. They watched as Neil Armstrong stepped onto the moon's surface. He pressed his left foot into the dusty ground. Then he spoke these famous words: "That's one small step for (a) man, one giant leap for mankind."

People all over the world watched the Apollo 11 moon landing.

For many people, this moment was more important than the space race. It was bigger than just exploring the moon. For them, this was a turning point in human history. One person, who watched the landing as a child, remembers wondering: "*Wow, what are we going to do next?*" The possibilities for science and exploration seemed unlimited.

Neil Armstrong carried a camera and took pictures of Buzz Aldrin and their surroundings.

The astronauts collected about 47 pounds (21.3 kilograms) of moon rocks and dust to study back on Earth. They also planted an American flag. It had a rod through the top. That way, it looked like it was flapping in the wind even though there was no atmosphere on the moon.

CAMERAS IN SPACE

When Armstrong exited the LM, he pressed a lever on the outside. This released a TV camera. Inside the LM, Aldrin flipped a switch. Now, the camera could beam video back to Earth. The pictures were picked up by tracking stations on Earth. The moon landing is considered the most important television event of the 20th century.

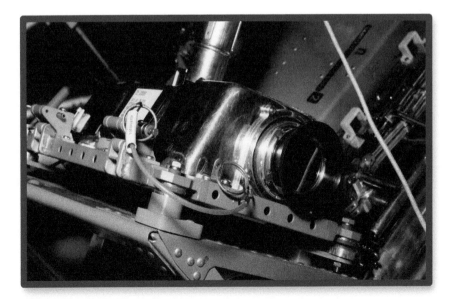

The TV camera that recorded and transmitted video of humankind's first steps on the moon

CHAPTER 4

RETURNING HOME TO A CHANGED WORLD

The astronauts spent just 21 hours on the moon. Then it was time to return to Earth. The LM's engine lifted it above the moon's surface. The LM docked with Columbia. Collins was waiting for them. Armstrong and Aldrin came aboard Columbia. The astronauts **jettisoned** the LM, leaving it behind. Columbia fired **thrusters** and began the four-day journey back.

The LM returning to Columbia as Earth appears above the moon's horizon

After landing in the ocean, the Apollo 11 crew and a U.S. Navy diver floated in a raft as they waited to be picked up by a helicopter.

As they approached Earth, the astronauts turned Columbia. Its heat shield now faced the surface. When they were ready, the astronauts jettisoned the service module. Then Columbia started downward through the atmosphere.

The temperature outside reached 5,000 degrees Fahrenheit (2,760 degrees Celsius). The heat shield protected the astronauts from the intense heat. The astronauts made it through safely. Once they were back in Earth's atmosphere, parachutes opened. Columbia floated gently into the Pacific Ocean. This type of landing is called a **splashdown**.

Moon rock

Moon rocks collected during the Apollo 11 mission were carried in special containers to NASA laboratories for study.

Apollo 11 changed the world. Scientists studied the moon rocks and dust brought back to Earth. This helped them learn about geology and even about the early history of Earth. Studies are still going on today. NASA scientists developed powerful new technologies to get Apollo 11 to the moon. For example, they used computers that were new at the time. The Apollo program helped push the technology forward and develop new computers.

The success of Apollo 11 gave NASA confidence to try more missions. In the following decades, NASA developed the space shuttle. It sent rovers to Mars. NASA sent a probe to Pluto. It also launched the Voyager missions to explore faraway space.

The spacewalk also made people from all nations feel unity. As Michael Collins said, "The thing that really surprised me was that everywhere we went people didn't say, 'Well you Americans finally did it.' They said, 'We did it.' All of us together, we did it. It was a wonderful sensation."

Perseverance rover landed on Mars in 2021.

The Cold War continued until 1991. But astronauts from the United States and the Soviet Union began to work together. Soviet cosmonauts and American astronauts **collaborated** on the Apollo-Soyuz Test Project. This was the world's first international space mission. The project paved the way for more international missions. Now we have an International Space Station.

FACT

The International Space Station has had a crew on board since 2000. More than 242 people from 19 countries have visited the station.

In 1975, the U.S. Apollo capsule and the Soviet Soyuz spacecraft docked in space.

International Space Station's crew members from the United States, Russia, and Japan posed for a photo in 2021.

Going to the moon seemed like an impossible goal. But President Kennedy said America would be there within a decade. With the help of many minds and hands, it happened. Apollo 11 showed that by working together, humans can accomplish incredible things.

TIMELINE

OCTOBER 4, 1957: The Soviet Union launches Sputnik 1, the first artificial satellite.

AUGUST 19, 1960: The Soviet Union launches Sputnik 5 with two dogs on board. This is the first mission to send living beings into space and bring them home alive.

APRIL 12, 1961: The Soviet Union sends the first human into space.

SEPTEMBER 12, 1962: President John F. Kennedy declares publicly that Americans will reach the moon before 1970.

SEPTEMBER 17, 1962: NASA announces the New Nine. These astronauts will focus on getting to the moon.

FEBRUARY 3, 1966: Soviet Luna 9 lands on the moon. It does not carry any living beings.

JUNE 2, 1966: U.S. Surveyor 1 lands on the moon. Like Luna 9, it does not have a crew.

DECEMBER 21, 1968: U.S. Apollo 8 sends the first human beings to the moon. It orbits the moon and returns to Earth safely with three astronauts aboard.

JULY 16, 1969: Apollo 11 launches from Cape Canaveral.

JULY 20, 1969: U.S. astronauts Neil Armstrong and Buzz Aldrin walk on the surface of the moon.

JULY 24, 1969: Apollo 11 crew splashes down in the Pacific Ocean.

JULY 17, 1975: U.S. and Soviet spacecraft dock, or link together, in space. The Apollo-Soyuz project is a success.

DECEMBER 26, 1991: The Soviet Union collapses. The Cold War is over.

NOVEMBER 20, 1998: The first piece of the International Space Station launches into space.

GLOSSARY

astronaut (AS-truh-nawt)—a person who travels to outer space; often, they have studied science and mechanics

collaborate (kuh-LAB-uh-rayt)—to work together

command module (kuh-MAND MAH-jool)—the main part of the Apollo spacecraft, where astronauts lived and worked

cosmonaut (KAHZ-moh-nawt)—a person from the Russian space agency who travels to outer space

jettison (JEH-tuh-suhn)—to throw or drop something away from an aircraft or spacecraft

life support (LIFE suh-PORT)—systems that help astronauts stay warm and breathe when they are away from Earth

lunar module (LOO-nur MAH-jool)—the part of Apollo 11 that made the journey from lunar orbit to the moon's surface; also known as the "LM" or Eagle

service module (SUR-viss MAH-jool)—the part of a spacecraft that holds oxygen, fuel, and power to keep astronauts alive and the spacecraft running

splashdown (SPLASH-down)—landing a spacecraft in water, using parachutes

thruster (THRUH-stur)—a small engine on a spacecraft that is used to move the craft in outer space

READ MORE

Fabiny, Sarah. *What Is NASA?* New York: Penguin Workshop, 2019.

Spilsbury, Richard. *Space.* North Mankato, MN: Capstone Press, 2019.

Woolf, Alex. *Neil Armstrong: First Man on the Moon.* New York: Random House, 2019.

INTERNET SITES

NASA Science: Space Place
spaceplace.nasa.gov

National Geographic Kids: The Moon Landing
kids.nationalgeographic.com/explore/history/moon-landing

Penguin: 10 Out-Of-This-World Facts About the Moon Landing
penguin.co.uk/articles/children/2019/jul/facts-about-moon-landing-space-race-apollo-11.html

INDEX